Putting God's house in order

Good stewardship of resources is an important responsibility within the life of local churches. Within every church, however large or small, there are committees, groups and individuals charged with the responsibility of ensuring that resources of money and property are cared for and used wisely.

This section includes pages of information and ideas for these people. **Please split it up between them.**

Applying these suggestions will help you to "*put God's House in order*", to save money and to make a positive contribution towards caring for the whole of creation.

The different parts are printed on separate sheets for ease of distribution, even though this uses more paper!

You will find **sub-sections** on:

Church Buildings
The Manse
Church Land
Money
Shopping and Catering

All these matter a lot to us in the church, but they must be looked at in the light of the Gospel, for

where your treasure is, there will your heart be also.

Matthew 6.2

Number 12 of the ROOTS and BRANCHES pack from The United Reformed Church, 86 Tavistock Place, London WC1H 9RT

Church Buildings –

heat and light

In a typical church, the cost of running and maintaining the property is the second most expensive item after the cost of ministry.
Among the costs, the **energy bill** is an expensive annual item.

By their nature, churches are unique buildings:
- ► They tend to be large, with high ceilings;
- ► They often have a regular but infrequent use;
- ► They are probably fairly old without any provision for energy conservation.

These factors mean that specialised professional advice is needed to maximise the savings that can be obtained on a church's energy bill.
The 1998 URC General Assembly instructed the Church & Society Committee to work on a plan to enable churches to undertake energy audits for their churches.

But even without such professional advice, there are some positive ways of reducing your church's energy bill without losing any comfort.
These include:
- ☑ Fitting low-energy light bulbs where possible.
- ☑ Only heating rooms that are actually being used.
- ☑ Where possible arrange room bookings to maximise the use of the premises in any one day. It is **much** cheaper and better to heat the premises for a whole day and have meetings and activities using them, than to heat the premises on successive days for individual separate bookings.
- ☑ Consciously remember to shut doors and to switch off unnecessary lights, with polite notices to encourage this.
- ☑ Fit draught-proofing strips around doors.
- ☑ Repair broken windows immediately to minimise draughts and heat loss.

Easy steps towards saving money and saving the earth!

Manse matters

One of the ways that a church can exercise good care of its property, its minister *and God's creation* is to keep the manse in good order.

In addition to normal routine repairs or decoration consider the following practical environmentally-friendly measures.

Renewing

When replacing windows, avoid frames made of tropical wood from non-sustainable sources.

When replacing a boiler, choose an energy-efficient 'condensing gas boiler' which will save fuel so lessening the contribution to global warming.

Upgrading

Energy conservation saves money and helps to save the planet!

☑ Ensure that the loft insulation is at least 6 inches (15cm) thick.
☑ Fit draught excluders to doors and windows.
☑ Consider installing cavity wall insulation.
☑ Install thermostats on radiators.
☑ Lag the hot water tank with a jacket.
☑ Install low-energy light bulbs.

Both Local Authorities and the energy utilities should be able to advise on the availability of grants for energy conservation measures.

Changing the manse?

If you are changing or purchasing a manse, consider the following factors:

☑ Can you minimise your minister's motoring by locating the manse carefully?
☑ Is the location also served well by public transport?
☑ Is the proposed manse an energy-efficient home?

Deceptively easy steps towards saving money and saving the earth!

A Churchyard

or church land

The Psalmist sings: "The earth is the Lord's". This earth includes even the land around your church building, whatever its size, tiny or vast.
Sometimes church land is perceived as a problem but with planning and effort a bare patch can be turned into a fitting tribute to the Lord of creation.

Some pointers for sustainable land use:
- ☑ Start by making a plan of the space available, noting area of shade.
- ☑ Consider how you could use the space:
  - ► is it just to look at?
  - ► is it accessible for sitting in?
  - ► could it be an area for play or other activities?
- ☑ To encourage wildlife plan to plant native species and provide wildlife stations for nesting or feeding.
- ☑ A grassy area can be turned into a wildflower meadow.
- ☑ The garden will be easier to manage if you avoid fast growing species.
- ☑ Avoid using peat.
- ☑ Consider having a compost area for church waste.

See also the suggestions given in the Children's Work section 14

Additional Resource
The Living Churchyard Pack is a resource with a wealth of additional ideas aimed at churches with larger areas and particularly for those with graveyards.
This may be obtained from The Arthur Rank Centre, National Agricultural Centre, Stoneleigh Park, Warwickshire. CV8 2LZ

Deceptively easy steps towards saving money and saving the earth!

Money

Investing

If you are involved with investing some of the church's money, then it makes good sense to put it where it will do some good - this is called ethical investment.
The national trusts of the URC have adopted some simple criteria for avoiding damaging or hypocritical investment.
Local churches and Provincial Trusts should follow this lead.

> *"Shares or securities of companies whose main activities are in*
> 1 the manufacture of alcoholic drink
> 2 the manufacture of tobacco products
> 3 the provision of gambling facilities
> 4 the production of armaments
> *are to be excluded."*

Beyond this policy of avoidance there is an opportunity to be more positive. There are a number of investment funds which select companies according to positive environmental criteria.

Banking

Churches often keep a sizeable amount of money in their local bank which does give an opportunity to ask the bank some questions about its environmental stance, e.g.
☑ *Do you have an environmental policy?*
☑ *What environmental charities/schemes have you supported?*
☑ *Do you consider the environmental impact of a project before agreeing a loan?*

The 1992 General Assembly of the United Reformed Church actually passed a resolution touching on this subject:
"Assembly welcomes the ethical policy statement of the Co-operative Bank. We support and encourage this development and urge the principle on all commercial and industrial undertakings."

Raising funds

Holding a Jumble Sale is an environmentally-friendly venture. Not only does this raise funds for your church but it actually encourages recycling and reuse!

Deceptively easy steps towards saving money and saving the earth!

Shopping and

Catering

Churches, like individuals, make choices when going shopping. If your church wanted to promote care for God's creation, consider the following shopping list and catering guide:

Shopping Check-list

☑ Fair Trade: Where possible always choose fairly traded products. Most good supermarkets now stock fairly traded tea, coffee (instant and filter) and chocolate, all of a high quality. Producers ensure that damage to the environment, for example by pesticide use, is minimised and that workers are not exploited. Look for the independently monitored *Fairtrade mark* (>>). Consider running a Traidcraft stall in your church.

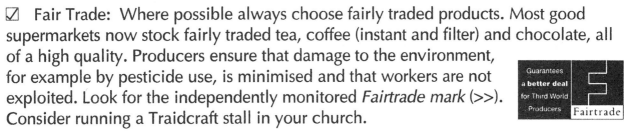

☑ Organic: Buying organic produce really is better for you and for the planet.

☑ Local: Buying locally-produced items actually benefits the environment as it minimises the energy consumed by transportation

☑ Recycled: Choose recycled paper products for your writing or printing, and when purchasing kitchen rolls or toilet paper.

☑ Envelopes: Use 're-use' stickers or the manila (brown) envelopes which involve less harmful bleaching.

☑ Cleaning: Choose environmentally friendly cleaning products where possible. Avoid chlorine-based bleaches, phosphate-based detergents and any cleaners that are not 100% biodegradable.

Catering

☑ Use your church's china wherever possible and avoid 'throw-away' cups and plates. Washing up your china is good for fellowship and avoids needless waste!

☑ Ensure that used paper, cans, glass and plastics are recycled. Almost everything can be recycled these days. Waste vegetable and plant matter can be composted.

(see also the checklist, Section 11A)

Deceptively easy steps towards saving money and saving the earth!

ROOTS and BRANCHES pack *from The United Reformed Church, 86 Tavistock Place, London WC1H 9RT*

3   We Believe ...

From time to time Church people have gathered under the guidance of the Holy Spirit to consider the beliefs of the Church and sometimes to formulate these beliefs into a creed.

During the fourth century in order to define what were core understandings and beliefs for Christians, various meetings (Councils) were held, including one at Nicaea out of which came the Nicene Creed. You can find this at 760 in Rejoice and Sing.

The United Reformed Church accepts with thanksgiving such declarations of faith from the past but is always open to God's guidance in making new statements of faith. One of the great challenges for the 21st century is to live in such a way that the quality of life for our descendants will not be impaired.

Can you draw up a creed which outlines our belief in God the creator and states our responsibility to exercise care for Planet Earth?

4   A FURY Covenant   *nothing to do with money or tax relief!*

After the flood the Bible records that God made a promise to all living things on earth:
God said to Noah: 'I am now establishing my covenant with you and with your descendants after you and with every living creature that is with you, all birds and cattle, all the animals with you on earth, all that have come out of the ark.
I shall sustain my covenant with you. Never again will all living creatures be destroyed by the waters of a flood; never again will there be a flood to lay waste the earth.' Genesis 9. 8-10

As a sign of this covenant Genesis records that God made the sign of the rainbow.
In the light of your environmental concerns, prepare a 'Rainbow Covenant' for your church to make with the Creator, using appropriate words and images. Display this covenant on a poster or banner. Move it to a different position after a couple of months.

5   Getting the message across

A Dramatic Sketch: Bring some life to your Church with a dramatic sketch. The example included in the 'Roots and Branches' pack was used with strong FURY input at the 1998 General Assembly. Better still, write your own.

Gabriel's Report: Inspection is a part of lives. Everything from your local butcher's shop to your school is subject to an inspection from time to time. Just imagine for a moment that the angel Gabriel is returning to earth to inspect its condition.
What observations would the report make?
What recommendations might be offered to the Church world-wide?

Check out other sections of 'Roots and Branches'

☑   the 'View from the Planet Doctor' and the other fact sheets in the 'Roots' section
☑   the Activities and the Children's Work sections suggesting some other ways to turn your environmental concerns into positive actions

FOOTPRINTS
for FURY

Pooh and Piglet go hunting and nearly catch a Woozle
from a story by A. A. Milne.

One fine winter's day when Piglet was brushing away the snow in front of his house, he happened to look up, and there was Winnie-the-Pooh. Pooh was walking round and round in a circle, thinking of something else, and when Piglet called to him, he just went on walking.
"Hallo!" said Piglet, "what are you doing?" "Hunting" said Pooh.
"Hunting what?" "Tracking something," said Winnie -the- Pooh very mysteriously.
"Tracking what?" said Piglet, coming closer. "That's just what I ask myself. I ask myself: What?"
"What do you think you'll answer?" "I shall have to wait until I catch up with it," said Winnie-the-Pooh. "Tracks." said Piglet. "Paw-marks." He gave a little squeak of excitement. "Now, look there." He pointed to the ground in front of him. "What do you see there?"
"Oh, Pooh! Do you suppose it's a - a - a Woozle?"

(© extract from 'Winnie the Pooh' reprinted by permission of Methuen Children's Books a division of Egmont Children's Books Ltd.)

Environmental Footprints
As Pooh and Piglet walked round in a circle on a snowy day, they left a trail of footprints. The footprints showed where they had been and the mark that they had left.
The concept of the environmental "footprint" is similar. Our environmental footprint indicates both where humans have been active and the activities that they have been involved in.
We all leave an environmental footprint. It is a part of life that whilst some of our footprints, like those of Pooh and the Woozle may vanish in the melting snow, other footprints leave a longer-lasting impression.

Your Church's Footprint
Governments, companies and churches leave environmental footprints but most are unaware of their impact.
This section, Footprints with FURY, contains a number of ideas and suggestions to help you assess your church's footprint and to consider whether your church tiptoes gently through the year or stomps through the seasons leaving deep tracks where it has trod?

So take a look through all the ideas and then choose where to begin.

Number 13 of the ROOTS and BRANCHES pack from The United Reformed Church, 86 Tavistock Place, London WC1H 9RT

1   Assessing our Footprint

Tick which your church comes closest to -

How much energy does your church use on heating?
☐A   Jesus was born in a barn and it feels as if we worship in one too.
☐B   Our energy bill is through the roof, which is also where much of our heat goes too.
☐C   Our church is comfortable, thanks to good insulation and careful use.

How brightly do your lights burn?
☐A   The church is lit at a level so that we can just about read the hymnbook but can't see the dust.
☐B   The wattage of our lights means that they double up as our heaters, summer and winter.
☐C   Our church has low-energy light bulbs providing good light without costing a fortune.

Is your church involved in recycling?
☐A   The last time recycling was mentioned was in our Guild when one of the members reminisced about her penny farthing.
☐B   We had a policy on it once, but we think that it got filed.
☐C   Our church chooses recycled paper products and has a collection point for material that can itself be recycled.

How often do environmental issues get mentioned in your church?
☐A   Not since 'All things bright and beautiful' was expunged from the hymnbook.
☐B   It usually gets a mention at harvest time and the yard out the back where all the rubbish gets dumped was once called our wild patch.
☐C   It is a concern of our Finance & Property Committee who have brought some positive proposals forward and we often have a 'green' perspective to our Sunday worship.

How did your church score:

3 or more As   - *so the 20th century has passed you by!*
3 or more Bs   - *lots of potential but could try a lot harder!*
3 or more Cs   - *you are ready for a Church Green Award!*

2   Reducing the Footprint

How to tip-toe through the tulips

If your church scored 3 or more C's, give yourselves a pat on its back and then g
busy sharing these ideas with neighbouring churches.
But if - more likely - your church scored 3 or more A's or B's then it's time to pu
God's house in order literally and locally.

Three steps to environmental heaven:

Step 1   **Assessing the Situation**
Make an environmental audit of your church's footprint and brainstorm possible ways of reduci
this imprint.
Use the Environmental Checklist from this 'Roots and Branches' pack to help you.

Step 2   **The PLAN**
By now you should have an imaginative list of ways forward. These need to be brought together
a plan. Draw up a list of proposals and, if possible, work out where environmental and financial
savings can be made. It may be that the whole package will look more attractive if those ideas
which require some effort or expenditure have a payback. Base your proposals on real figures - t
always looks impressive to those charged with financial matters!

Step 3   **Policy & Action**
To turn your ideas into action, first look for people in your church who might offer support. If yo
church is taking 'Roots and Branches' seriously over a year or so, you should be able to put your
ideas in the church magazine or newsletter or on the notice-board and ask the worship leader to
have more 'green' themes in worship. (Different things work best in different churches.)
Then bring your proposals to a church meeting and gain the agreement in advance of those who
will be able to turn policy into action to help save God's earth - and save the church some money
in the long term.
Do your very best to ensure that your plan will not join the mountain of great ideas gathering dust
the back of the vestry cupboard!

and why not set up an Environmental Taskforce?

Could your FURY Group form an environmental taskforce to undertake a piece of
conservation or other positive environmental work for your church or local community?
If you want to do something in your local community consider contacting your County
Wildlife Trust or a similar body through your local authority to see if they can involve you in a
particular project. It might be that you can offer your labour or could help raise funds to plant a tree
or small wood.

Don't forget:
☑   Consult your URC 'Good Practice' pack!
☑   Contact the local press; they like local stories with photo-opportunities.
☑   Invite your non-church going friends along to get involved.

Assembly big bang!

Roots and Branches presentation staged at

URC General Assembly 14th July 1998

Parts:
Narrator - dressed normally at a lectern or out of sight with microphone
Boss - smart suit and appearance
Technician- boiler suit and general scruffy appearance, smoking if allowed
Four or five assistants - walk-on only, any clothes! Only one is required to manoeuvre the balloon if the protective sheets can be laid down in advance.

Props:
Large (at least 24") blue balloon with green outline of continents roughly sketched onto it with a green felt-tip pen or paint
Spray paints: red, black, blue and brown
Strips of paper and / or assorted small pieces of rubbish in a bucket or waste paper basket
'Spraymount' type glue
Large plastic sheet or decorator's sheets, to protect the floor
Bamboo cane (6' or 8') and cord or string to suspend the balloon over the stage area
Cigarette with a pin in the end to help burst the balloon

Caution: be sure to open windows or other ventilation as this sketch involves spraying paints in an enclosed space.
Best to have a full rehearsal, including sacrificing a balloon!

If the balloon sketch goes well, try another - write your own or adapt this one:

Cookery Demonstration: A Recipe for Disaster
1) *Take more than we need*
2) *Combine with all the waste products*
3) *Pop on the stove and ignite*
4) *Turn up the heat*
5) *Continue adding more to satisfy our taste until there is little left*
6) *Argue about the flavour*
7) *Pop in the oven*
8) *Discuss the time to bake .... It is burnt, it is finished.*

Number 13A of the ROOTS and BRANCHES pack from The United Reformed Church, 86 Tavistock Place, London WC1H 9RT

Narrator: Once upon the time there was a big blue planet. It was suspended in space like a glistening sapphire and was beautiful to behold.

- *Action*   *The planet is brought on, suspended from the cane. The other assistants bring on a large protective sheet which lies under the planet, unless this can be positioned in advance.*

Narrator: The big blue planet teemed with life, green plants with flowers of every colour in the rainbow, waters teeming with flashing silver, the air filled with a myriad of song and across the land slithered, walked, ran and crept many, many living creatures.

- *Action*   *Technician enters and surveys the planet*

Narrator: Among these creature was the human species, made in the image of God and who, from time to time, acted as if they were God.

- *Action*   *Boss enters and greets the technician*

Boss: This planet looks very dull, let's have some development. Get rid of some of that forest to make room.

- *Action*   *Technician sprays green areas brown.*
- *Action*   *Boss surveys the planet with appreciative noises.*

Boss: That's better, a bit of variety in the world, and we didn't need all those bugs and beetles. Now we need some real progress. Let's go for the oil, gas and coal.

- *Action: Technician paints black dots across the seas and sprays the surface of the planet with patches of red.*
- *Action*   *Boss surveys the planet with appreciative noises.*

Boss: What's a bit of global warming when we can get all this energy, what's a bit of oil pollution when we can go where we want.
We need growth, that's the key. Let's build factories to make more goods, lots of things. The more people buy and consume, the richer we will become.

- *Action*   *Technician sprays glue (spraymount) onto the planet, then throws coloured paper over it. This should stick to the glue and paint. Then the technician pours a bucket of assorted rubbish, e.g. small pieces of orange peel, bottle-tops etc. over the planet. These should fall to the ground with a clatter.*
- *Action*   *Boss surveys the planet with appreciative noises.*

Boss: That's better, a bit of development, some real wealth, and why should we worry about the mess. Where there's muck there's brass.
Now you, you've worked hard, take a break, have a cigarette.

- *Action*   *Boss offers Technician a cigarette. Technician takes one and lights it. Slowly and purposefully takes a drag, blows the smoke and simultaneously moves hand with cigarette away from mouth until it touches the balloon with a bang!*

Seeds and Saplings

Ideas for children's work

Things to do indoors

1)   Creating Planet Earth

Make a papier maché globe pasting strips of newspaper onto a blown-up balloon. If you use wallpaper paste, take care as most of them contain a fungicide. PVA glue is quite safe. Once the model is dry, paint it and suspend it from your ceiling.

2)   Create an environmentally-friendly Garden of Eden:

Make a Garden of Eden collage out of scrap or recycled materials pasted onto a large piece of cloth or card. Display it in the church porch with a coloured-in Roots and Branches sign.

3)   Poster Activity

Make a poster together featuring everyone's favourite animal, flower, bird or insect and add a message about caring for the world. The poster could be displayed specially or at the harvest festival.

Something to do outdoors

A Lenten and Easter Garden

If you have a little bit of garden or land at your church, you could plant a Spring Garden.

☑ In the autumn buy some snowdrop and daffodil bulbs.

☑ When you are ready to do your planting, dig a shallow trench in the shape of a cross.

☑ Place the smaller snowdrop bulbs down and across the centre of the cross.

☑ Then, leaving a space around these snowdrop bulbs, plant the daffodil bulbs a bit deeper all around the edge of the cross.

☑ Once you have planted the bulbs, put the soil back and wait for Spring!

You should have two beautiful displays, one of bobbing snowdrops during Lent, then, as Easter comes, some daffodils should appear to trumpet the resurrection. The bulb garden can grow under grass if the turf is removed prior to digging the shallow trench and then replaced following planting. To ensure a display year after year, allow the bulb leaves to die back naturally.

Number 14 of the ROOTS and BRANCHES pack from The United Reformed Church, 86 Tavistock Place, London WC1H 9RT

The Story of St Francis

Francis was born about 800 years ago in Italy. His family owned a cloth business which made them quite rich. As a young man Francis joined the family business until an illness changed his whole life. After he got better he left the family business and set out to help the poorest people in a life of Christian service. Some people thought that Francis's new way of life was so special that they decided to join him. They became known as Franciscans. Francis didn't just care for people. He saw that everything that God had made in creation was very special. So special, in fact, that he thought of the other parts of creation as his own family. Francis called the sun: 'brother sun' and the water: 'sister water'.
(see also the poem by St Francis in the anthology, Section 8, and in Rejoice & Sing, 39)

Let's ask ourselves:
What is your favourite bit of the world God has made?
Is it an animal or bird (which one)? A fish or insect? The sea or land? A mountain or river?

Storytime

The story *"In the Beginning"* is on a separate sheet (14A) for ease of reading together.

After the story, let's ask ourselves:
Do we like what God made?
Do we think that we take care of God's world?
How do we think that we could take better care of it?

Beasty Bugs Prayers

THANK YOU GOD
FOR SPOTTED LADYBIRDS
FOR WONDERFUL SPIDERS
FOR BEES IN TREES
AND FOR ALL THOSE SLIMY CREEPY CRAWLIES
THAT LIVE UNDER ROCKS.

AMEN.

This is just one example of a 'Beasty Bugs' Prayer.
Let's write or draw our own prayers?
We can pray these prayers with eyes open or with actions.

Storytime

IN THE BEGINNING . . .

A long, long time ago, before the wind blew and the sun shone, there was a silent emptiness. God was sad. Then God decided to fill it with something good.

First, God made a big bang and out of the bang, lots of stars appeared. They whizzed through the space like giant balls of light. Then God made a switch. God called the off-switch, 'night' and the on-switch, 'day'.

Then God got really busy. God took all the hard bits from the big bang and made them into round shapes like balls. God called one of them Earth. The bits in between were sky and space.

It was starting to get really exciting . . .

Number 14A of the ROOTS and BRANCHES pack from The United Reformed Church, 86 Tavistock Place, London WC1H 9RT

On Planet Earth God made some bits dry, which were called land and other bits wet, which were called rivers and seas.
The sea would be really handy for the fish that would come soon.

Next, God decided that the earth needed a bit of life.

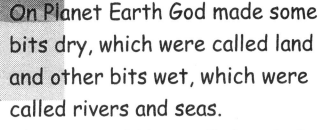

Soon little bugs started to grow and the Earth came alive. After the bugs, came plants and trees, fish and birds and then every sort of animal.

God looked and was delighted in all that was there. But God thought for a bit, and decided that there was something missing in the world.

hello

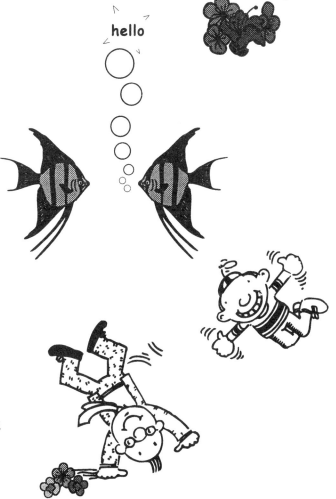

Can you guess what?
Yes, God decided to make people like you and me.
God said to the humans:
I would like you to take care of all the world, of all the plants and animals and all the living things.

The Roots and Branches
Hymn Board

Daily doth the almighty giver
bounteous gifts on us bestow;
his desire our soul delighteth,
pleasure leads us where we go.
Love doth stand at his hand;
joy doth wait on his command

God's great goodness aye endureth,
deep his wisdom, passing thought;
splendour, light and life attend him,
beauty springeth out of naught.
Evermore from his store
new-born worlds rise and adore.

from All my hope on God is founded, RS 586
Robert Bridges (1844-1930) based on Joachim Neander (1650-1680)
from the Yattendon Hymnal, by permission of Oxford University Press

The following is a selection of other hymns which express worship to God the creator, praise for the creation or concern with human stewardship.

All numbers from Rejoice and Sing

All creatures of our God and King 39
Creator of the earth and skies 82
Father Eternal, Ruler of Creation 624
For the beauty of the Earth 41
For the fruits of all creation 42
For the healing of the nations 620
Glorify the Lord (A Song of Creation) 737
God in his love for us lent us this planet 85
God who made the earth 62
God who spoke in the beginning 60
God, who stretched the spangled heavens 86
God, whose farm is all creation 612
How great is your name, O Lord (Psalm 8) 670
I love the sun 65
I sing the almighty power of God 43

Immortal, invisible, God only wise 67
Lord, bring the day to pass 87
Lord of the boundless curves of space 44
Morning has broken 45
Now join we, to praise the creator 89
O come, and let us to the Lord (Psalm 95) 707
O Lord, all the world belongs to you 90
O praise him! 46
O worship the king 47
Praise and thanksgiving 48
Praise, my soul, the King of heaven 104
Praise to the Lord, the Almighty, 74
Praise ye the Lord, 50
The universe to God in silence sings 122
Think of a world without any flowers 123
To God who makes all lovely things 52

Other hymnbooks with suitable items include The Big Blue Planet and worship material from the Iona Community; all available through URC Bookshop.

Rooting God's Word

A Set of Bible Studies exploring the theme of creation.

Week by week people gather to worship God.
In the Reformed tradition worship is centred around God's word in the Bible, listening, reflecting and considering its message today. These Bible studies are offered as a resource for use within your church to consider the theme of creation.

Many people, whether within or outside the church, have some preconceptions about the biblical stories of creation. For some, the story of creation, though difficult, is understood as a literal truth which can leave us with an inadequate 'Sunday School' picture book image of God.
For others, there is an underlying suspicion that science has won and the Bible has become an irrelevance. Placed alongside the 20th century theory of the 'Big Bang' and the widely accepted account of the evolution of species a literal understanding of the creation stories can leave us worrying that the Bible has little to offer our technological world.
This set of Bible studies is intended as an antidote to such views. Through five Bible studies we will explore who God is, think about our relationship to God, consider our place in the created order and our responsibility for the environmental challenges that the world faces.

The studies are drawn from five different parts of the Bible:

1: Gardening stories ...	A look at the creation stories in Genesis
2: Teaching Creation ...	Drawing some lessons from the Pentateuch.
3: Singing Creation ...	Psalms as a source of praise for creation.
4: Good News for Creation ...	Some insights from the gospels.
5: Dear Creation ...	Exploring New Testament letters.

These Bible studies in 'Roots and Branches' are primarily offered for use within a housegroup or other Bible study meeting. However, they could also be used as resource material for preparing a series of sermons or by individuals.

PTO

Number 16 of the ROOTS and BRANCHES pack from The United Reformed Church, 86 Tavistock Place, London WC1H 9RT

A few hints for arranging a Bible Study:-

- Ensure that you have appointed someone who will prepare the study and be able to guide the group through it.
- If you are meeting in a home, try to ensure that the study leader doesn't have to act as the host as well.
- In addition to publicising the event, it is a good idea to offer people personal invitations.
- At the start of the session make sure that everyone knows each other. Refreshments at this stage often get a gathering off to a good start.
- Offer prayer at the beginning of each session
- At the end, consider asking what people and issues it is appropriate to remember in the closing prayers.
- Try to ensure that no one dominates the meeting and that everyone is invited to contribute.

1 Gardening stories

Step 1 An Introduction
Gardening is growing in popularity, a sign of which is the increasing number of programmes dedicated to gardening on television. Not only can we learn how to grow and nurture flowers and vegetables through the seasons, but now we are encouraged to plan and redesign our gardens- it is almost as if we are becoming a nation of Capability Browns!

Step 2 For Discussion
Ask if anyone present has any experience or stories or even dreams about planning a garden or a section of a garden from scratch? Ask people to talk about planning the garden, doing the work, the feelings that people have as the garden takes shape and when it is finished. Ask also about what is necessary to keep the garden in good order.

Step 3 Looking at the first creation story
In the Bible there are two different versions of creation given in the opening chapters of Genesis. We might understand these as planning a garden on a planetary scale! In the same ways as two biographies of the same person can complement each other and give us a bigger picture, so these two stories of creation can give us a bigger picture of God as creator and our relationship to both God and creation.
The first one, which describes the six days of creation is laid out rather like a responsive reading that might be used in church. *Read Genesis 1. 11-23.*

Imagine this passage being read in worship with the congregation replying with the refrain: "And God saw that it was good."
For discussion
What does this refrain tell us about how God looks at creation?
Does this refrain have any implications for those who use the garden?
Does this give us any insight into the relationship between God and God's people?

Step 4 Looking at the second creation story
If the first passage is laid out like a reading in worship, the second version reads more like a story. The whole story runs from Genesis Chapter 2 verse 4b to Genesis chapter 3 verse 24 and includes both the account of creation and the fall. We are going to concentrate on the account of creation. *Read Genesis 2.4b - Genesis 2.25.*

For discussion
Are there any similarities with the stories which your group have told about gardening from scratch?
What does the story say about God?
What does the story say about creation?
What does the story say about our relationship to God and responsibility for creation?

Finally- a challenge
Church buildings are often designed so that people know they are a place where God is worshipped. Steeples, towers and crosses all act as symbols of a gathered church. If you have a patch of land, however small, outside your church, brainstorm how your church patch might be redesigned to express an understanding of God and the place of humans in creation that you have just discussed.

see also sections 7 and 14 of Roots and Branches

2 Teaching Creation....

Drawing some lessons from the Pentateuch.

Step 1 An Introduction
This study examines some passages from the first five books of the Bible, known as the Pentateuch. These books contain stories and teachings whose aim is to encourage the readers to live as faithful people of God. This Bible study will explore attitudes to land to see what wisdom can be gained for use today.

Step 2 For Discussion
We view and use land in many different ways. Discuss why we value the different types of land listed below and what responsibility we feel we have for their care:

1 *A garden owned by freehold.*   2 *A rented allotment.*
3 *Common or 'wilderness' land such as the Dartmoor National Park or a beach.*
4 *National Trust land open by entrance fee.*   5 *A tropical forest.*
6 *A piece of land which you particularly value.*

Step 3 Exploring the Pentateuch
Land is a crucial resource to the people of God. In the Pentateuch we can discover how the issue of land is related to ethics and God. The ideas which we can draw out of the Bible are sometimes theological ideals, but they do represent a significant challenge to God's people, yesterday and today, in their struggles with land issues.

a) Land as a Divine Gift: read Deuteronomy 26. 1-12.
For the People of God, the promised land was the fulfilment of the process of salvation that began with the exodus from Egypt. Whilst in the wilderness they were given guidance as to how they should treat the land that they had been promised. Sadly, stories in the Bible and from current affairs reveal that this gift of God has been the subject of dispute and violence.
What do you think the people of God gained from their wilderness experience?
How might we develop relationships which respect land, people and our God?

b) Resting the Land: read Leviticus 25. 1-5 & 8-15.
In Genesis 1 we read how God values the Sabbath as a time to rest. In these verses from Leviticus we understand that the land is ordained a time of rest too, a common practice in many traditional societies.
What are the advantages of allowing land under production to rest?
In our growth-orientated world, does the concept of a Sabbath or imposing a limit on production have anything to contribute to the way in which we view land today?
Leviticus informs us that land belongs to God, and we, as tenants may only lease it.
What can an understanding of God as the Earth's freeholder contribute to our society?
If the earth belongs to the Lord... does land have a sacred quality?

Step 4 A Reprise
Remembering your thoughts about land in step 2, ask whether any of the Biblical concepts that you considered can contribute to our understanding of the care and use of land.

Step 5 A Task
Deuteronomy 26 includes a creed (Vs 5-10) which the people of God would recite in worship. Try writing a creed telling the story of a piece of land, or even the whole earth, including your responsibility for it.

3 Singing Creation

Psalms as a source of praise of creation

The collection of psalms is the song book of the people of God in the Old Testament. It is filled with Psalms that deal with all aspects of faith and life including expressing a sense of awe, wonder and understanding of God's creation and the human place within it. In this study we will explore some of these aspects.

Step 1: Creation hymns. Look up some of your favourite hymns that mention creation as a topic- what do they tell us about the created order? *(Section 15a lists some hymns of this theme)*

Step 2: Psalm of Creation. Read Psalm 104, which seems to interweave the creation story from Genesis 1 with the contemporary surroundings of the people of Israel. In doing so the psalm gives a dynamic quality to creation as bearing witness to God's continuing activity rather than a one-off act. Thinking of parts of creation that you have visited, have you ever sensed that God's creating activity continues? Share your thoughts.

The story of God's creation is told in many different ways in the Bible. Whilst some account have a more historical feel this Psalm is written as a song to sing and affirm. It is not only a song that the people of God sing, but it seems to affirm that the whole of creation from the sun and moon to the storks and lions are joining in this song of praise. This song of praise by the whole of creation can be a challenge to the human-centred attitude which people can have of creation. If we sense that the rest of creation is singing in praise to God, does that alter our view and attitude towards creation?

Step 3: Psalm in crisis. Look up Psalm 74; It may be helpful to read this Psalm aloud in three sections, pausing in between. Before reading the psalm introduce the verses as follows:
1- 11 A lament of a national catastrophe.
12-17 Remembering the saving acts of God in the past.
18-23 Restating the continuing activity of God before the people in worship.

This psalm seems to allude to the destruction of the Temple of Solomon by the Babylonians. It may help to identify with the psalm if you recall a national catastrophe, people's reliance on God who has helped in the past and placing their hope in God who will guide them into the future.
Now look again at verses 12-17.
What is the particular saving activity that is remembered by the people of Israel to give them confidence that God will see them through the current crisis?

It is interesting to read that this psalm records God's purpose of bringing about salvation being first understood through creation itself. In the Christian Church we particularly identify God's gift of redemption through Christ. Does creation take on a new value because it speaks of God's saving love?
Does this make any difference to our attitude towards creation?
Does this make any difference to our Church life?

Step 4: Reprise
Return to one or two of those hymns that you chatted about in step 1. Do you have any more to add about their understanding of creation following the Bible study?
If you were to introduce one of these hymns in Church on Sunday, what would you say about it to the congregation?
Close by singing one of two of your favourite creation hymns.

4 Good News for Creation

Some insights from the Gospels ...

Step 1 Discussing Lifestyle

Lifestyle is a buzz-word of the 1990's. Our first study drew on the growing popularity of garden design, but this is only one aspect of our increasingly life-style orientated world. Week by week magazines articles and television programmes bombard us with lifestyle 'musts' from the latest look in fashionable clothes to designer kitchens, from the colour of our eggs to the design of a room. Colour supplements include articles about so-called media personalities under such titles as 'A day in the life of...' or 'My favourite room by....'. How do you feel about such articles?

Step 2 WWJD?

A new acronym has entered the Christian vocabulary from America- WWJD? It stands for What Would Jesus Do? Imagine that you have to compile a colour supplement article under the title 'A Kingdom Lifestyle by Jesus of Nazareth'. Discuss key features of the lifestyle of Jesus that you would include.
Some suggested texts for reference include: Matthew: 6. 19-21, 24-31, 7. 24-27, 8. 20, 10. 29-31.
You might even like to write it out, or consider appropriate locations for a photo-shoot!

Step 3 Impact

Different lifestyles are said to give us particular benefits, a beer and chips diet might enhance our girth and it is said that our choice of clothing or a car can make a statement about who we are. Our lifestyle choice can also influence our lives and the environment! Consider one or two lifestyles including your own, and the Jesus Kingdom style above; and for each one discuss the impact of following it on the environment and our personal well-being.

Step 4 Change

We understand that Jesus lived in a very different context to ourselves. 2000 years ago there were no mobile phones and e-mail was as fast as the nearest donkey. But there are many similarities - people are still concerned about relationships, healing, forgiveness, debt, food, isolation, poverty and other key issues. What environmentally-beneficial features (i.e. good news!) of the lifestyle of Jesus are you attracted to? How is it possible to translate them into our life as the 21st century dawns?

Step 5 Church lifestyle - More Good News for Creation

The Gospel according to John opens by mirroring the first verses of Genesis: *'In the beginning...'.* In doing so John links the person of Jesus with God from the beginning of time. As the good news unfolds in John's gospel, it is clear that God is eternal yet begins a whole new relationship with people through Jesus. John develops this train of thought in chapter 15 as he discusses Jesus' teaching on the vine and the branches. The passage builds on the Old Testament understanding of God as the vinedresser and Israel as the vine; we may understand it as an intimate picture of the Church and Christ. *Read John 15. 1 - 5.* Building on the gardening imagery, what parts of Church life would you prune and what parts would you encourage to fruit, that creation might bloom?

Number 16d of the ROOTS and BRANCHES pack from The United Reformed Church, 86 Tavistock Place, London WC1H 9RT

5 Dear creation ...

Exploring New Testament Letters...

Step 1 Paul's letter to the Romans

Consider the average letters page in the URC Reform magazine. The letters present cover a number of styles and topics. There are letters dealing with issues which divide and letters of encouragement, there are letters questioning and letters stating a viewpoint. The letter of Paul to the Christians at Rome is no different. It opens with a greeting, then deals with his understanding of the way that God offers to redeem people through belief in Jesus Christ in both a supportive and challenging way.   *Read Paul's letter to the Romans Chapter 8. vs. 1-25.*

Step 2 Causes and Consequences

"For we know that up to the present time all of creation groans with pain, like the pain of childbirth." Rom. 8. 22

In the style of the 'Consequences' party game, invite each person to write in the centre of a piece of paper an environmental issue which might cause creation to 'groan'. Next, invite each person to consider a cause of the environmental problem identified, then to identify one cause of the cause. These are to be written above the issue. Then, invite each person to write down one possible consequence of the environmental issue and then a consequence of the consequence stated. Write the consequences below the issue. Then share your analysis. Have you identified any common causes of the various environmental problems identified? Do the potential consequences of the issue heighten the need to make changes?

Step 3 Struggling for the Kingdom

It has been said that many of our environmental problems stem from an economic system that is reliant on growth and trade and which needs military power to ensure its safety. It is also said that such an economic system responds positively to the greatest profit margins, which themselves may be generated by exploiting labour or not paying the true environmental costs of production.

It is natural for humans to want to look after their own interests. Most churches prefer to have a healthy bank balance rather than one teetering towards nothing! *Look again at Romans 8. 5-10.* Discuss whether you think that there is any link between the current groaning of creation and the dilemma which Paul identifies of putting our faith in the Spirit or in human nature.

Step 4 Hope for the Future

Christian hope is not about escapism but is based on the understanding, symbolised in baptism, of dying to an old way of life and rising transformed to a new way. Such hope is invaluable because it frees us from fatalism and a sense of hopelessness in the face of the current ecological crisis. *Read Romans 8. 19-21.* This passage affirms that God is not only our God of the past but also our God who precedes us into the future.

If you have identified problems with human nature or the prevailing economic system, list some measures which would help to alleviate these problems?

Step 5 Dear Creation ...

Write a letter to a person or organisation of your choice and suggest one positive step that could be taken to bring a little more hope to our environmental concerns.

Think Globally
Act Locally

Roots & Branches

MEMORANDUM:

to: Any United Reformed Church
from: Leaders of 179 Nations
dateline: Rio July 1992

We write to invite your church to help us care and nurture this planet.
From today we need to plan and act to ensure that the needs of all of today's generation of people are met without preventing the needs of tomorrow's generation being met too. Some say it cannot be done.
Imagine that you are in a large Ark called Planet Earth. Instead of having two of every creature on board as in the story of Noah, you have the whole created order!
The challenge is to manage the finite stocks and renewable resources so that present and future generations can have a share. You need to make sure that the world we leave will be habitable by our children's children. It is a tall order, and one that requires thought and action.
The whole process is called Agenda 21, which has been agreed by us all here.

We depend on your response.

signed ... A - Z

PS It won't be an unfamiliar role; Christians have made a responsible contribution to society for 2000 years. Though the role is familiar, the agenda is new.

AGENDA 21 - one key to local community action

It involves individuals and groups working with their Local Authority Agenda 21 Group to make a difference.   *Some ways forward*:
* Ask your Local Authority about their plans for Agenda 21.
* Ask how you or your church can become involved.
* Discover what other local groups are doing for Agenda 21.
* Plan a positive action.
Refer to Section 4 in 'Roots'

Could your church do something too?

Thinking Globally ... Acting Locally

Think Locally - Act Globally!

THE UNITED REFORMED CHURCH HAS A MEANS TO DO THIS, TOO.

The *Commitment for Life* programme enables local churches to link with partner organisations to help fulfil the words of Jesus: *I have come that they might have life, and have it abundantly.* (John 10.10) *Commitment for Life* is concerned when environmental issues have a negative impact on people's lives.

Water is a major issue for our Commitment for Life partners.

In Palestine the availability of water is an issue of justice. The average Israeli uses over three times as much water as the average Palestinian - and pays much less per litre.

The water problem *in Bangladesh* has roots in poor environmental management and basic poverty. This nation, surviving on a low-lying delta, is subject to flooding from both land and sea. From the land side there have been increased incidences of sudden floods which have been attributed to tree-felling on the slopes of the Himalayas. From the sea side there is an increased risk of marine incursions because eroded banks leave the nation more vulnerable to the storms and rising of the sea-level associated with global warming.

In Zimbabwe the water problem results from severe shortages and erratic rainfall, the latter being attributed to the effects of El Niño.

In Salvador, Brazil, only a small minority in the shanty towns have fresh water in their homes or a sewage system

COMMITMENT FOR LIFE **is about making hope real.**

- *In Palestine*, PARC are conducting research into water conservation techniques. E.g. recent trials have shown the benefits of using waste water from a fish farm as liquid manure.

- *In Bangladesh*, the CCDB Partner is working to provide safe water and sanitation, especially in flood-devastated areas.

- *In Zimbabwe*, training is given by Silveira House in various water conservation techniques, the building of small dams, simple irrigation systems and water purification systems.

Thus, supporting *Commitment for Life* is all about ...

Thinking Locally ... Acting Globally
Thinking Globally ... Acting Locally

COMMITMENT FOR LIFE fits well with ROOTS AND BRANCHES

more information from Commitment for Life, 86 Tavistock Place, London WC1H 9RT

ACTIVITIES

Things to affirm and to do

Roots & Branches

Throughout this Roots and Branches Pack there are various suggestions of things to affirm and do.
This 'pick & mix' selection is a repeat of some with some extras suggestions. It is intended that these might become a springboard for your own creative ideas.

Things to Affirm

1 Making a Covenant

The Old Testament is full of covenants, or agreements between the people and God. Sometimes God makes an unconditional covenant with Israel, for example, after the flood when God promises never again to destroy the earth. God also gave a rainbow as a sign to mark this covenant. Sometimes God makes a conditional covenant, for example, in Exodus 34 from verse 10, where God promises to work wonderful miracles if the people will obey a set of laws.
Consider making a covenant which is appropriate to your local church.
For example: *God promises ...*   *St Francis's URC promises ...*
Such a covenant could form the focal part of a service of worship and could include promises from various parts of your church life, especially those who have been working on the 'Roots and Branches' sections. The covenant could be marked by a sign and displayed in your church.
(See also the suggestions for FURY in section 13)

2 Ten Commandments

Devise 10 appropriate Green Commandments for your church.
The following is a list of some suggestions:
1) Run a recycling point at your church.
2) Change ordinary light bulbs for energy-saving ones.
3) Choose recycled paper products for church stationery and recycle your waste in (1) above.
4) Insulate your loft, water tank and draught proof windows and doors.
5) When filling the church kettle, use only as much water as you need.
6) When travelling to church, walk when possible, use a bus where available or share lifts.
7) Fix leaking water taps to prevent waste.
8) Fit thermostats to radiators.
9) Organise a collection day for unwanted spectacle glasses and shoes.
10) Turn down your thermostat by 1 degree - surprisingly, this will save up to 10% of your fuel bill.

You could turn your ideas into a sketch to use with Moses and God on Mount Sinai.

Things to Do

Hold a Jumble Sale

It is a great way to recycle what is no longer needed and you can raise valuable funds. If you wanted to hold a really 'Green' Jumble Sale, aim to appropriately recycle all the items not sold and use the profits that you make in an appropriate way.

Hold An Unusual Recycling Day

Many people will be familiar with the location of Local Authority sites where glass, paper etc. can be recycled. Consider having a day where more unusual items are brought for recycling. Examples include spectacles, shoes and Christmas cards. Your efforts can make a very positive contribution to another community.

Jam Jar Day

Consider holding a jam jar day once a quarter. The idea is that people bring along empty jam jars and others take them away to make jam/chutneys. The next jam jar day people can bring back their full jam jars for sale and collect some more empties to refill.

Car Sharing

In an ideal world we would either walk or use public transport to get to church. Life is not that simple and many people rely on cars to join in worship or attend a meeting. Ask someone to organise a car sharing list which people can sign either requesting or offering a lift. Don't be too ambitious when you start, or why not do it once on a special Sunday and award people fun stickers if they managed to share a lift that day.

Write a Letter

Share your environmental concerns with the wider world. Consider writing a letter to a politician in your Local Authority or the UK Government. Letters may have more effect if you indicate that your church is willing to make a commitment and that you hope the politicians will too.
For example:
to the Local Authority:
Our church is concerned about recycling. If you would provide a place at such and such location for recycling, we will commit ourselves to using it on a regular basis.
to the local MP or Prime Minister:
Our church is concerned about global warming. We will undertake to fit low-energy light bulbs throughout our premises. Will you, in turn, pledge to remove VAT from certain energy-saving products to encourage their use?

Local Agenda 21 *(see also section 4)*

Every Local Authority should have an Agenda 21 programme. Why not invite a speaker from your Local Authority along to a Church Meeting to find out what is happening and how your church can play a part?

...nd Reusing Paper

...ld scrap paper be used in taking notes/minutes or for children's work?

...s your church collect paper for recycling?

...g

...s your church only use china crockery, glasses and metal cutlery?

...ou recycle glass, tins and aluminium cans?

...rt

...s your church encourage and enable car-sharing?

...s your church have provision for the secure storage of bikes?

...sing and Sales

...s your church choose recycled paper in the office, toilet and kitchen?

...s your church use biodegradable cleaning material where possible?

...s your church have a Traidcraft stall and hold jumble sales?

...& Property

...re many possibilities to minimise your church's environmental impact when undertaking ...g or repairs. **See also section 9.**

...you plan for the maximum level of insulation and avoid tropical hardwood?

...your church use ethical criteria in any invested funds?

...area within your church grounds managed for the benefit of wildlife?

...you banned the use of peat and considered having a compost pit in the grounds?

...mmunity

...d your church become involved in a local environmental group or venture?

...faith and the environment

...could your church most meaningfully link the Christian role of taking care of planet earth ...n the worshipping and learning life of your church?

Checklist

This section is in two parts.

First, there is a questionnaire which you can use to gain a snapshot picture of your church's use of resources.

Second, there are some ideas for you to consider as a church which may help you save money and improve the prospects for God's earth.

The Environmental Snapshot

Energy
Fill in the two tables below to discover how much money your church spends on energy and how much energy has been used each year for the past 3 years.

		£ Spent (in hundreds)		
	Years ago	1	2	3
Heat Source: Coal				
Oil				
Gas				
Electricity				
Other				

		Units of Energy consumed (in kilowatt hours)		
	Years ago	1	2	3
Heat Source: Coal				
Oil				
Gas				
Electricity				
Other				

Paper
How much money did your church spend on paper stationery last year?

How many reams of paper and number of envelopes does this represent?

Catering
How much does your church spend annually on disposable plates, cutlery and cups?

Transport
How many cars are used on an average Sunday to transport people to church?

What is the average occupancy rate of the cars?

How many people walk or cycle to church?

How many people get to church by public transport?

Purchasing and Sales
How much toilet paper and cleaning materials does your church use in an average year?

Finance & Property
Is your church planning an extension to its building?

What sum of money does your church have invested or in deposit accounts?

What church grounds does your church have?

Local Community
What local links to community organisations does your church have?

Linking faith and the environment
On what occasions in the worship of your church were environmental issues
    mentioned during the past year?

Reducing the Impact

Use the following checklist to highlight where savings can be made.

Check against your snapshot to see the potential annual impact, financia
Some suggestions apply to manses as well as to church buildings.

> THIS IS A SUMMING-UP SECTION.
> PLEASE REFER TO OTHER SECTIONS FOI
> INFORMATION, IDEAS - AND INSPIRATION

Energy CONSERVATION

Does your church have:
☑ Draught-proofing around window frames?

☑ Loft insulation? If yes, is it at least 150 mm (6 inches) thick?

☑ Lagging around hot water pipes and tanks?

☑ Effective door closers on external doors?

Energy REDUCTION

☑ Does your church use low energy light bulbs where possible?

☑ Is your church heating controlled by thermostats in each room?

☑ Are time switches used for heating and lighting?

☑ Do you have 'please switch-off unnecessary lights' signs?

Energy EFFICIENCY

☑ Is the boiler regularly serviced?

☑ If your energy use is relatively constant or if it varies, can you identi

It is hoped that the United Reformed Church may follow the example
and introduce an advisory service on energy matters for local churche

Using
☑ Co

☑ Do

Cateri
☑ Do

☑ Do

Transp
☑ Do

☑ Doe

Purcha
☑ Doe

☑ Doe

☑ Doe

Financ
There a
buildir

☑ Can

☑ Doe

☑ Is ar

☑ Hav

Local C
☑ Cou

Linking
☑ How
  with

INTRODUCTION

Roots & Branches

Over the last few decades
some new words and phrases
have crept into our language:
Silent Spring and *Torrey Canyon* in the 1960's
Three Mile Island and *Seveso* in the 1970's
Acid Rain and the *Ozone Layer* in the 1980's
Global Warming and *Greenhouse Gases* in the 1990's

Each of them spell an environmental threat and each of them can leave us with a sense of sorrow and unease about the earth we are bequeathing to our children and our children's children. This unease is felt from individuals right up to national leaders.

1992 witnessed the largest ever gathering of world leaders in Rio, Brazil for the Earth Summit. One of the key messages from the Earth Summit was that environmental problems cannot be dealt with by Government leaders alone.

Every citizen needs to play their part too.
'Roots and Branches' is a contribution to this process from the United Reformed Church.

The aim of the pack is twofold.
Firstly, to help churches develop an understanding of the Christian imperative to have awe and care for what we know as God's creation.
Secondly, the pack is to help enable individual churches to make their life of worship, witness and mission as environmentally-friendly as possible.

The focus in this pack is on the local church.
It is hoped that a follow-up pack will be produced to encourage and enable each of us as individuals to make a difference by changing our personal life-styles.
But for now, let's 'green' our church and do our bit for God's wonderful earth!

... 'Roots and Branches' ... putting God's house in order.

Number 1 of the ROOTS and BRANCHES pack from The United Reformed Church, 86 Tavistock Place, London WC1H 9RT

What are the Roots?

The 'Roots' are the basic resources on which this pack draws.

Roots include elements of our Christian tradition which have something to say about God's creation and our responsibility for it. These faith 'roots' embody Biblical passages, theological understandings, and writing drawn from our Christian heritage to the present.

Roots also include some very basic information about the Planet Earth, some vital statistics, a health check and a glossary of environmental terms.

What are the Branches?

The 'Branches' are the place where the ideas bear fruit, where the action takes place.

Branches include activities in our church like Worship, Children's Work, Management of Property and Finance, Catering, Social or Fellowship Groups.

Within this pack there are 'branches' for many parts of the life within your church; not all will be relevant to YOUR church.

Each of these branches contains some ideas for reflection and action.

Getting Started

Step 1   Receive the pack at your Church Meeting.

Step 2   Take the loose-leaf 'Branches' and distribute them amongst the appropriate groups within your church.

Step 3   Ask each designated group or individual to consider the material, drawing on the 'Roots' sections as needed.

Step 4   Invite them to report back their branch's ideas at a future Church Meeting, probably in 12 months' time.

Step 5   Begin to formulate appropriate environmental targets for your church.

Step 6   Report your decisions and experiences to the Church and Society office.

To get the best out of the pack it is recommended that your church appoint either one person or a small group to encourage and guide them through the whole process.

If the Holy Spirit flows like sap from the roots to the branches,

then the leaves on the tree will be for the healing of the nations.

Summit for the coming generations

In 1992 the largest ever gathering of national leaders took place in Rio, Brazil. The unprecedented event which motivated so many politicians to gather together was the United Nations Conference on Environment and Development, known as the **Earth Summit.**

The Summit had origins in a gathering of 70 Governments in Stockholm in 1972 which established the United Nations Environment Programme (UNEP). UNEP's main task was to ensure that Governments take more care of Planet Earth.
Through the 1980's it was recognised that in addition to protecting the earth, it was also vital to meet the needs of development for all the world's peoples. To deal with these two issues in an integrated way the UN established the Commission on Environment and Development which produced a report entitled 'Our Common Future' and established a new goal, that of **sustainable development.**

Sustainable development is about people having a quality in their life, both in our generation and in those that follow, for it respects the necessity to meet the needs (which is not the same as desires) of today's people without compromising the ability of tomorrow's generations to live.

The Earth Summit helped to move this concept towards a programme of action. At Rio a number of important proposals were made including:
- a climate change convention to deal with the threat of global warming;
- a convention on desertification;
- a biodiversity action plan with the aim to value both species and the habitats in which they live.

A further step was the establishment of the *Agenda 21* **Programme.**
Agenda 21 is a blueprint for our planet's survival, a set of ideas to be put into action for the 21st Century. For *Agenda 21* to work government and industry, organisations (including churches) and each citizen must play their part.

Adopting this approach in our world today

will make life tolerable for our children.

Number 4 of the ROOTS and BRANCHES pack from The United Reformed Church, 86 Tavistock Place, London WC1H 9RT

View of a
PLANET DOCTOR

Patient Name: Earth

Date of Birth: approximately 4600 million years ago.
First signs of life: approximately 3000 million years ago.
First sign of human life: approximately 100,000 years ago.

Development of Patient:

The planet has developed at a steady rate over the years, with the evolution of micro-organisms, an atmospheric system, a water system and plant and animal kingdoms. The case history indicates some unexplained problems including the extinction of dinosaurs. The planet has also coped with a 'flu-like' cycle, where it has moved over time from warm, sweaty periods to much colder times known as ice ages. These variations are consistent with the observed solar system cycles. However, the planet has appeared particularly stressed in recent decades and so was referred to the Planet Doctor for a check-up.

Symptoms and Diagnosis

Weight Loss:
This planet, like so many bodies, has reserves of fat which act as a part of its survival strategy. Unfortunately, these fats, which are deposited in solid coal, liquid oil and gas have been subject to acute liposuction, so rapidly reducing these reserves which took millions of years to form. Apart from resource depletion, this radical surgical technique has other harmful side effects including temperature increase and water problems.

Running a Temperature:
This is a problem that has taken some 250 years to diagnose. There is now a clear view amongst planet doctors that the planet's atmospheric temperature is rising, principally as a consequence of burning fossil fuels which has produced a measurable increase in the concentration of carbon dioxide in the atmosphere.

The symptoms are:
- *changes in climatic conditions*
- *more storms, floods and droughts*
- *a rise in sea level*

The prognosis is grim for it appears that the burning of oil is addictive. Unless the patient can be weaned off this drug, then a fever will result.

Lung Disease:

For millions of years the planet has breathed through its forests, one of its vital organs. Each leaf within the forests breathes in carbon dioxide and releases oxygen, maintaining a fresh air life-giving cycle. Unfortunately, it is clear that human activity has increasingly destroyed the planet's lungs over the past 5000 years, and particularly at a fast and increasing rate through the twentieth century. This lung disease threatens the ability of the Planet to maintain a fresh air cycle.

Water works:

The planet is suffering from water retention problems. Symptoms include the sea whose level is rising and the land, where some temperate areas are becoming semi-arid and some semi-arid regions are becoming deserts. This condition is a consequence of rising temperature and the lowering of the water table because of increased extraction.

Halitosis:

The planet has suffered from halitosis for the past 250 years. The problem has developed along with a process called industrialisation which is associated with the human organism which lives on the planet. The effects include damage to surface tissue and to the buildings which the humans are developing. The human organism suffers with asthma and lung disease as a consequence.

Thinning:

The planet's protective layer of ozone is clinically shrinking. As with the loss of any tissue layer, this renders the planet's human inhabitants liable to increased incidences of fatal skin cancer and cataract problems.

SUMMARY Diagnosis and Prognosis:

"The patient is suffering from a cancerous-like growth of the human organism. Unless the current human activity changes, the prognosis could prove critical for the prospects of any life of this planet."

signed off: *Dr Solomon*

VITAL statistics

The UK Environment- A Dynamic Picture

Wildlife:

Between 1969 and 1993 the populations of 19 species of birds including the corncrake and capercaillie fell by over half. Butterflies are also in decline with 5 species becoming extinct and 18 suffering a drastic decline over the last 150 years.

Hedgerow:

Between 1947 and 1993, 418,000 kilometres (260,000 miles), which represents over half our hedgerows, were grubbed up.

Land:

Between 1945 and 1990 over 700,000 hectares (1,730,000 acres) of rural land was urbanised. This is an area larger than Greater London, Berkshire, Hertfordshire and Oxfordshire combined.

Farmland Birds:

Skylark numbers have declined by over half in the last 25 years.

Rivers:

There is mixed evidence that the water quality in some rivers is improving, but in others it is declining.

Beaches:

In 1993, 93 beaches out of 457 failed to meet the EU bathing water directive because of high levels of sewage pollution. This is a slight improvement on previous years.

Fish Stocks:

Cod stocks in the North Sea are now 1/3rd the size that they were in the early 1970's.

Carbon Dioxide Emissions:

At present, it is apparent that the UK will return to the 1990 levels of carbon dioxide emissions by 2000. It is widely accepted that further reductions are needed to minimise the impact of global warming.

Air Quality:

Nitrogen Oxides, which contribute to photochemical smogs, have increased over the last 20 years, mainly as a consequence of the increase in traffic.

Timber Imports:

The UK imports 87% of its timber requirements, mainly from forests that are not managed sustainably.

source: Green Gauge report from the Environmental Challenge Group sponsored by RSPB and WWW

Recognising our loss is a step towards change.

Planet EARTH
- as God sees it

Roots & Branches

In the beginning ...

The very first stories in the Bible are filled with layers of meaning which affirm God as creator of the whole universe and which stress the privilege and responsibility that humans bear within the created order.

God the Creator

The story of creation is an account of origins, not the origin of God, but of God's activity. God's activity is revealed in the beginning when God set in motion a process pregnant with possibilities.

Light shone, form shaped, spirit breathed and life danced, all of it tumbling out of the created order. Creation was the act through which life could begin. "In the beginning" reveals that the Earth belongs to the Lord.

And God saw that it was good ...

The story of creation is written as a song of celebration, with a recurring refrain:

"God saw that it was good."

The refrain underlines the concept that all of creation including plants, sea creatures, birds of the air, animals - small and large - as well as the human race have value in God's sight.

Christians therefore believe that since God values something, then it is for Christians to value it too.

God saw that it was good ...

a call to those created in the image of God to keep creation looking good in God's sight.

Number 7 of the ROOTS and BRANCHES pack from The United Reformed Church, 86 Tavistock Place, London WC1H 9RT

Be fruitful and multiply, fill the earth and subdue it ...

The interpretation of this verse *(Genesis 1, 28)* is a key to understanding human responsibility within creation.

In the Journal *Science* in 1967, Lynn White asserted that "Christianity bears a huge burden of guilt" for the damage inflicted on nature. Lynn White claimed that the understanding to 'fill the earth and subdue it' or to 'have dominion' has been interpreted as a licence to exploit creation at will. Lynn White's article, which has been the subject of much criticism, expresses a fear about one extreme interpretation.

But there are other interpretations of this verse.

One traditional understanding of 'having dominion' means the exercising of good stewardship. In this sense the role of the human becomes planetary caretaker. However, some feel that this 'management style' understanding is too human-centred and risks neglecting the value of other species in the eyes of God.

Another image, which some theologians claim is a rediscovery of the original meaning of the text, is that of a good sovereign who has dominion over land and subjects. A good sovereign exercises dominion with respect for land and people.

[see also the sections on Worship (15) and Bible study (16)]

However the verse from *Genesis* is interpreted, it is clear that acid rain, global warming, deforestation, desertification and various other environmental ills are not a sign of having dominion, but of losing it!

Taking a leaf

If "the leaves on the trees are for the healing of the nations" (Revelation 22 v 2), so some of the leaves from books written later than the Bible may illuminate the process.

This section, "Taking a leaf", is a short anthology of writings gathered down through the centuries. It is here to inspire, to stimulate reflection - and to be added to.

Irenaeus Bishop of Lyon (c. 130-c.200)

"In the beginning God fashioned Adam, not because he had need of human beings, but so that he might have beings on whom to bestow his benefits."

"God made man lord of the earth, but he was small, being but a child. He had to grow and reach full maturity."

"Thus there is one God the Father, and one Christ Jesus our Lord who came in fulfilment of God's comprehensive design and consummates all things in himself."

The legacy of the writings of Irenaeus reveals a figure, whom against the background of the rejection of the material world, strongly affirmed the involvement of God in the creation of the whole created order. Moreover, he affirms the positive role of Christ as someone who came not to reverse the fall of Adam and Eve in Eden, but instead to seal God's commitment to the world.

Columba (c.521-597)

"By the divine powers of the great God is suspended the globe of earth and thereto is set the circle of the great deep supported by the strong hand of God Almighty, promontories and rocks sustaining the same, with columns like bars on solid foundations immovable like so many strengthened bases."

"Delightful l think it to be in the bosom of an isle, on the peak of a rock, that I might often see there the calm of the sea. That I might see its heavy waves over the glittering ocean, as they chant a melody to their Father on their eternal course."

Columba, Irish monk and missionary, journeyed to Iona on the west coast of Scotland from where he engaged in missionary work and wrote poetry. He lived a life close to nature and his writing reveals a person in awe of the glory of the God and yet aware that he, like all matter, was part of the ebb and flow of the created order. The influence of Columba is felt in Celtic Christianity, most notably in the contemporary Iona Community.

Hildegarde of Bingen (1098-1179)

"As the Creator loves his creation so creation loves the Creator.

Creation, of course was fashioned to be adorned, to be showed, to be gifted with the love of the creator. The entire world has been embraced by this kiss."

Hildegarde of Bingen wrote in the period following the darkest of times in the Middle Ages and a period in which Christianity was under the strong influence of Augustine. Against this background her mystical writing must have been a wonderful tonic. Through her words she expressed the sheer love of God for creation, a love portrayed as a mother's love for her child.

Francis of Assisi (1181-1225)

The Canticle of Brother Sun

Most high, all powerful, all good Lord!
All praise is yours, all glory, all honour and blessing.
To you, alone, Most High, do they belong.
No mortal lips are worthy
To pronounce your name.
All praise be yours, my Lord, through all that you have made,
And first my Lord Brother Sun,
Who brings the day; and light you give to us through him.
How beautiful is he, how radiant in all his splendour!
Of you, most high, he bears the likeness.
All praise be yours, my Lord, through Sister Moon and Stars;

All praise be Yours, my Lord, through Brothers Wind and Air,
And fair and stormy, all the weather's moods,
By which You cherish all that You have made.
All praise be Yours, my Lord, through the Sister Water,
So useful, lowly, precious and pure.

All praise be Yours, my Lord, through Brother Fire,
Through whom you brighten up the night.
How beautiful he is, how gay! Full of power and strength.
All praise be yours, my Lord,
through Sister Earth, my mother
Who feeds us in her sovereignty and produces

Francis was born into a relatively wealthy family but rejected his own background and chose a simpler, itinerant way of living, without the need for personal possessions. Through his life Francis gained a sense that each part of creation was a gift of God still filled with the very presence of God. It was a radically different perspective from the more utilitarian view of creation as the source of life's provision. Francis' great hymn, "The Canticle of the Sun", written in praise of God, extols his understanding of the relationship with God through every part of creation, including his brother sun, a line from which the hymn is named. The familiar hymn, "All creatures of our God and King", is a more recent version of Francis' hymn.

Julian of Norwich (c.1342- c.1415)

"And he showed me more, a little thing, the size of a hazelnut, on the palm of my hand, and round like a ball. I looked at it thoughtfully and wondered, "What is this?" And the answer came, "It is all that is made." I marvelled that it continued to exist and did not suddenly disintegrate; it was so small. And again my mind supplied the answer, "It exists, both now and for ever, because God loves it." In short everything owes its existence to the love of God. In this "little thing" I saw three truths. The first is that God made the earth; the second is that God loves it; and the third is that God sustains it."

Julian of Norwich was attached to St. Julian's Church in Norwich in the turbulent period following the black death. Whilst little is known about her life, her writings reveal a person aware of the great love of God and who has experienced the presence of God within each part of creation.

Chief Seattle (19th Century)

"Even the white man, whose God walks and talks with him as friend to friend, cannot be exempt from the common destiny. We may be brothers after all; we shall see. One thing we know, which the white man may one day discover - our God is the same God. You may think now that you own Him as you wish to own our land; but you cannot. He is the God of man, and His compassion is equal for the red man and the white. This earth is precious to Him, and to harm the earth is to heap contempt on its Creator The whites too shall pass; perhaps sooner than all other tribes. Continue to contaminate your bed, and you will one night suffocate in your own waste. ...

But in your perishing you will shine brightly, fired by the strength of the God who brought you to this land and for some special purpose gave you dominion over this land and over the red man. Your destiny is a mystery to us, for we do not understand when the buffalo are all slaughtered, the wild horses are tamed, the secret corners of the forest heavy with the scent of many men, and the view of the ripe hills blotted by talking wires. Where is the thicket? Gone. Where is the eagle? Gone. And what is it to say goodbye to the swift pony and the hunt? The end of living and the beginning of survival."

These words, drawn from a longer address are attributed to Chief Seattle of the Duwamish League. They were delivered in 1854 in response to a government proposal that reservations be established. The words are written as a prophetic warning from one people of God to another and as a lament which continues to be echoed in the words and songs of indigenous people the world over today.

Number 8 of the ROOTS and BRANCHES pack from The United Reformed Church, 86 Tavistock Place, London WC1H 9RT

Gerard Manley Hopkins (1844-89)

Binsey Poplars felled 1879.
My aspens dear, whose airy cages quelled,
Quelled or quenched in leaves the leaping sun,
All felled, felled, are all felled;
Of a fresh and following folded rank
Not spared, not one
That dandled a sandalled
Shadow that swam or sank
On meadow and river and wind-wandering
   weed-winding bank.

O if we but knew what we do
When we delve or hew -
Hack and rack the growing green!
Since country is so tender
To touch, her being so slender,
That, like this sleek and seeing ball
But a prick will make no eye at all,
Where we, even where we mean

To mend her we end her,
When we hew or delve:
After-comers cannot guess the beauty been.
Ten or twelve, only ten or twelve
Strokes of havoc unselve
The sweet especial scene,
Rural scene, a rural scene,
Sweet especial rural scene.

Gerald Manley Hopkins was educated at Oxford where he was influenced by the Oxford Movement. He joined the Roman Catholic Church and went onto become an ordained Jesuit Priest.

In 'Binsey Poplars felled 1879', he further explores the relationship between humanity and creation by painting a picture of regret and mourning following the destruction of some poplar trees. The loss is keenly felt by those who realised, too late, the beauty and vulnerability of creation and an experience which future generations would simply have denied to them.

Robert Runcie

"For centuries, far too many Christians have presumed that God's love is primarily directed at them, and that His natural order was created mainly for the use- and abuse - of humankind. Today such a man-centred attitude to our fragile and exhausted planet is at last beginning to look not only selfish and parochial, but also irresponsible and potentially disastrous. Hence all of us, especially Christians must open our eyes and minds wider still. We must realise that the way to maintain the value and the preciousness of the human is by re-affirming the preciousness of the non- humans also - of all that is. Indeed, the Christian God forbids the idea of a cheap creation, of a finite, dispensable universe. His universe is a work of non-expendable and ever-renewing love - and nothing that is fashioned in love must ever be regarded as cheap or secondary."
Lord Runcie, former Archbishop of Canterbury, wrote these comments in advance of the 1992 Earth Summit held in Rio.

Number 8 of the ROOTS and BRANCHES pack from The United Reformed Church, 86 Tavistock Place, London WC1H 9RT

John Polkinghorne

"In its course, science and theology have encountered each other in a way that seems, to me at least, to be characterised by fruitful interaction rather than mutual friction. Einstein once said, 'Religion without science is blind. Science without religion is lame'. His instinct that they need each other was right, though I would not describe their separate shortcomings in quite the terms he chose. Rather I would say, 'Religion without science is confined; it fails to be completely open to reality. Science without religion is incomplete; it fails to attain the deepest possible understanding.' The remarkable insights that science affords us into the intelligible workings of the world cry out for an explanation more profound than that which it itself can provide. Religion, if it is to take seriously its claim that the world is the creation of God, must be humble enough to learn from science what that world is actually like. The dialogue between them can only be mutually enriching. The scientist will find in theology a unifying principle more fundamental than the grandest unified field theory. The theologian will encounter in science account of the pattern and structure of the physical world a reality which calls forth his admiration and wonder. Together they can say with the psalmist:
"O Lord how manifold are thy works! In wisdom thou hast made them all."
John Polkinghorne FRS moved from being a professional physicist to an Anglican priest. It was a move which not only affected his daily life, but also led him on a journey of discovery into the relationship between the two disciplines with which he shared his life.
© **John Polkinghorne:** *Science and Creation - the search for understanding.* SPCK 1988

Al Gore

"My own religious tradition teaches me that we've been given dominion over the Earth, but that we must be good stewards of the Earth. We can't say, 'We didn't know. 'In the parable of the unfaithful servant, who is asleep when the thief ransacks his master's house, it is not enough for the servant to say, 'I was asleep, master.' Our home, our planet is being ransacked, We cannot plead ignorance. We are responsible. We have an obligation to respect life itself, an obligation to understand and respond to the inextricable links between justice and environmental protection. The issue is not just the greenhouse effect or the depletion of the stratospheric ozone layer or the loss of living species. The deeper issue is a change in the relationship between humankind and the ecological system of our planet. Industrial civilisation is on a collision course with the environmental system that supports life as we know it. The Earth's environment is crumbling in what seems like slow motion, in response to the onslaught of more and more people, and more and more technology, and more and more wilful environmental vandalism. The solutions we seek will be found in a new faith in the future which justifies action in the present, a new moral courage to choose higher values in the conduct of human affairs, a new reverence for absolute principles that can serve as guiding stars for the future course of our species and our place within creation."
Al Gore, Vice President of the United States of America, writes about the responsibility which our generation faces and he identifies the need for a new set of values in our understanding of the environment. It is a mandate for politicians and the people and a challenge to people of faith to take a prophetic lead.

GREENING
the church

In the last 50 years there has been an increasing world-wide concern with environmental issues.
Within the Church this concern has led to the development of a 'green movement' through which the links between the Christian faith and environmental issues are explored.

This section highlights three movements, one on a global scale, one at UK national level and one at an 'ordinary' local church.

The World Council of Churches:
Justice, Peace and the Integrity of Creation Process

The phrase Justice, Peace and the Integrity of Creation (J.P.I.C.) emerged from the Sixth Assembly of the World Council of Churches (W.C.C.) meeting in Vancouver in 1983. At the Assembly, delegates spoke with concern and conviction about a number of global and local concerns. As the delegates listened to one another they realised that the importance of environmental issues and that many of their concerns were inter-linked.

As a consequence the W.C.C. launched a process to covenant for Justice, Peace and the Integrity of Creation.
The W.C.C., in common with churches across the world, already had programmes on issues of justice and peace. The new emphasis that emerged in the J.P.I.C. process was the inclusion of the concern for creation and the interweaving of the concerns, one with another.

Throughout the remainder of the 1980's the W.C.C. sought to encourage churches and Christians to include the environmental agenda within their list of concerns and to integrate these concerns with other issues. The consequence was a process which brought a holistic and integrated dimension to church thinking. The whole process was underpinned by biblical study.

J.P.I.C encouraged Christians to link the cry of the oppressed in the scriptures with the cries that are heard today and to proclaim the message of liberty to captives which Jesus delivered in his manifesto for ministry (Luke 4. 16-21).

The legacy of the J.P.I.C. process includes the raising of the profile of environmental issues across the world church and the importance of making links between the issues and our Christian faith.

Number 9 of the ROOTS and BRANCHES pack from The United Reformed Church, 86 Tavistock Place, London WC1H 9RT

Christian Ecology Link

Today the Christian Ecology Link (CEL) is a body of approximately 500 Christians from across the nation who share an active interest in, and concern for, ecological issues.
The body had its origins in an informal prayer meeting of the
Green Party in 1981.
From its birth CEL rapidly grew into a network of people who aimed
'to spread ecological insights among Christian people and churches' *and*
'to spread Christian insights throughout the Green movement'.

CEL aims to work through individuals and local churches
where possible, by providing them with appropriate resources.
It keeps in touch with members through an annual meeting
with guest speakers, the publication of a quarterly journal
'Green Christians' and its news bulletin 'Caring for Creation'.
In addition, members are encouraged to meet in local,
ecumenical groups and to form denominational teams.

Two recent CEL ventures are aimed at enabling local churches to adopt a more sustainable life:

The first is a pack entitled *'Steps towards Sustainability'*, which deals with environmental issues on a topic basis. Within the pack is a wealth of information and ideas from Energy Use to Ethical Investment and Sustainable Eating to Sustainable Living. *(See Section 11, Resources)*

The second is a scheme designed to encourage churches to take some positive action. If a church takes 10 positive steps for the environment it may apply for
a **CEL Millennium Certificate.**
Herringthorpe URC, whose story follows, was the first church to gain the award.
The second was given to a Church of England Youth Group in Skipton known as *'On the Edge'*. Their activities included holding a fund-raising venture for the Yorkshire Wildlife Trust, using organic bread and fruit juice for refreshments at their club night and learning about animal welfare. The latter included a visit to a local vets' practice.

Through practical schemes and thought provoking resources, CEL encourages
both individual Christians and churches to think seriously about green
issues and to take some practical action.

For more information write to C.E.L., 20 Carlton Road, Harrogate, HG2 8DD.
or visit *www.christian-ecology.org.uk*

Herringthorpe United Reformed Church

In October 1997 this church in Rotherham became the first ever church of any denomination to be awarded a **C.E.L.** Millennium Certificate.

Ruth Holdsworth, who has been involved in the greening of the church from the beginning, tells the story:

"The start of greening Herringthorpe United Reformed Church began in January 1991, when the Church Meeting compiled a list of 'values to which the church commits itself and against which we can regularly review all proposals and progress'.

The sixth statement of seven states:
"We commit ourselves as a church to have a practical concern for the community and the environment locally and world-wide".
From then until 1994, the church was involved in major repairs to the building, due to subsidence, and this gave the opportunity for extending the premises as well. Environmentally concerned members of the church were able to put forward practical suggestions to the building committee at the earliest stages, so that a number of them were incorporated into the plans.

By 1994, when the building was complete, it was time to consider other green initiatives.
First of all a meeting was held for anyone interested in doing 'An Ecological Audit', using for guidance Sheet 11 of the 'Sustainability Pack' produced by C.E.L.
*The **EaRTH Group** (Environmental and Resources Thinking at Herringthorpe) was formed, and we considered where to start. We felt that we wanted to 'get our teeth into' something practical. Since then we have tackled a wide range of projects. A number are ongoing, like the monthly Traidcraft Stall, the periodical 'recycling days', improving part of the grounds for wildlife, and awareness-raising through items in the church newsletter, with information displays on the board dedicated to 'EaRTH matters'.*

Some things are one-offs, like leading worship on an environmental theme and holding a meeting on green issues to which we invited all the local churches. Sometimes we support ongoing national campaigns like Christian Aid's 'Change the Rules', and Jubilee 2000. While these are not primarily environmental, the 'spin-off' of improving conditions for people in the Third World is that the environment will also suffer less.

Not all of our initiatives have succeeded: an idea for a local authority mini-recycling centre did not receive approval, because of the possible problems of litter, broken glass, etc. But we are tackling recycling in a number of different ways with considerable success. We are learning that it is probably better to begin new initiatives gradually, so that those who are less convinced do not feel threatened by the changes. In the long term we hope this will be more effective.

Thinking green is slowly becoming part of the church's way of life. More people are becoming aware, and that is the first step. Then they need to be convinced that their contribution, however small, to improve the environment, is a further step in the right direction.

Eco-congregations!

In 1998 the Environmental Issues Network, which is a formal network of the Council of Churches for Britain and Ireland (CCBI), entered into partnership with *Going for Green*, Britain's biggest environmental awareness campaign. Together they have developed an Eco-congregation project, whose main objective is to help churches appreciate that environmental concerns are a core part of the Christian faith and to encourage churches to exercise good stewardship of the world's resources.

The Eco-congregation programme will work from the person in the pew through to denominational level to:
- encourage churches in positive thinking, worship and teaching to develop an understanding of the imperative to care for God's creation;
- enable churches to exercise stewardship of their resources, including buildings and land, according to best possible environmental practice;
- stimulate churches and church members to demonstrate their belief and commitment by working in and with their local communities for sustainable development, for example through Local Agenda 21;
- promote the establishment of environmental groups at all levels within churches;
- network with environmental groups, both within and outside churches;
- work with denominations in the development of an Eco-Congregation Award Scheme;
- encourage and enable participation by the churches in consultation with Government, industry and other bodies.

The Project is to begin in February 1999 and will be led by David Pickering, a United Reformed Church Minister, who will become the first Churches Environmental Project Officer. David's role will be to work with the URC and all other denominations on environmental issues.

For further information, help or advice please contact David at:
Going for Green
Elizabeth House
The Pier
Wigan. WN3 4EX
Tel. 01942 612621
Fax. 01942 824778
e-mail gfg@dircon.co.uk

The Environmental Issues Network was established in 1990 following the formation of the Council of Churches for Britain and Ireland and is a place to exchange information, ideas and resources and to reflect and comment on environmental issues.

Going for Green was created as part of Britain's response to the 1992 Earth Summit in Rio. Its environmental campaign, which is aimed at the general public, urges people to make small lifestyle changes which, if adopted by everyone, could help make a big difference to the future of the environment.

A guide to the JARGON

This Glossary includes a definition of certain environmental terms and in some cases a more subjective reference to the potential environmental consequences of the issue.

Acid Rain - the term used to describe the fall-out from the atmosphere of pollutants normally dissolved within rainwater but also as dry deposition. Acid rain is formed from the interaction of moisture with sulphur dioxide and nitrogen dioxide which derive from the burning of fossil fuels (coal, oil and gas), including vehicle exhausts. Acid rain affects water quality, causes the loss of vital nutrients from soil, damages vegetation including forests, scars buildings and has a detrimental effect on people's health.

Agenda 21 - an agenda developed for the 1992 United Nations Earth Summit (held in Rio, Brazil) and agreed by 179 Nations. Agenda 21 is meant as an 'Agenda for the 21st Century'. Its aim is to promote development which respects the environment and the needs of future generations. Whilst much of the responsibility for the development and implementation of Agenda 21 is at national level, each Local Authority is also required to develop a set of Local Agenda 21 policies promoting sustainable development. Local Authorities are required to consult people and interest groups, so local churches can play their part.

Biodegradable - indicates the potential of a substance to be broken down by the action of micro-organisms.

Biodiversity - literally means variety of life and refers to the number of different species and the richness of their interaction in any one place. One estimate suggests that there are 30 million different species living on earth. It is clear that just one of these species, the human, is threatening the habitats of many of the other species, thus reducing biodiversity both locally and globally.

Biosphere - that part of the planet from deep into the soil to high in the atmosphere in which some form of life is supported.

Biotechnology - the term used to describe technology that uses parts of living organisms to modify other living organisms or to create new organisms. Biotechnology can provide great benefits but its indiscriminate use without careful application and clear ethical criteria has potentially dangerous consequences. *See Genetic Engineering & Cloning.*

Chlorofluorocarbons (CFCs) - human-made chemical compounds used in a variety of applications including coolants in refrigerators. When released into the atmosphere they react with ozone to destroy it in the upper atmosphere. As CFCs are very stable, those released in this century will remain active in the atmosphere well into the next century. CFCs are also greenhouse gases, so their release contributes to global warming. *See Ozone layer and Greenhouse Gases*.

Climate Change - is a term generally used to describe the changes in climate at a local and global level as a direct consequence of global warming. The vast majority of scientists now acknowledge that Climate Change is a real phenomenon which threatens the well-being of creation. Its effects in different regions include more intense storms, more floods, more droughts- with a consequent loss in crop production and rise in disease.
See Global Warming, Greenhouse Effect and Greenhouse gases.

Cloning - the production of an organism with an identical genetic make-up.
See Biotechnology and Genetic Engineering.

Conservation - the management of a dynamic Eco-system in a sustainable way. Typically, an ecosystem may be managed to ensure that a particular species or group of species is able to flourish. *See Preservation*.

Deforestation - the action of cutting down forests in large scale operations, and is to be distinguished from sustainable forestry management. Deforestation often leaves fragile top-soil exposed to loss by weathering. *See Erosion*.

Desertification - a process whereby the loss of vegetation exposes productive soil so making it vulnerable to erosion. This process of desertification continues until only unproductive and infertile land remains. Desertification may be caused by climate change, drought and changes from traditional forms of land use to more intense production. Desertification leads to human poverty and drought. *See Erosion*.

Ecology - from the Greek word *oikos* which means house or place. It is the study of the relationship of living organisms with their surroundings. *See Environment*.

Ecosystem - a habitat in which different organisms interact and support each other. Eco-systems may be as large as a forest or a lake or as small as the life that exists under a damp stone.

El Niño - the name given to a set of phenomena which arise from climatic changes in part of the Pacific Ocean. The causes of El Niño are not fully understood but the consequences can be devastating for natural habitats and human communities world-wide.

Energy Efficiency - involves minimising the use of fuel whilst maintaining the positive benefit.

Environmental Science - the study of the interaction between humans and the natural system. *See Environment*

Environment - the context where humans interact with the natural system. *See Environmental Science*.

Erosion - the wearing away of material (e.g. soil or rock). Erosion occurs naturally and may be induced or speeded up by human activity.

Extinction - the loss of a species forever, an example being the Dodo. It is a natural part of the evolutionary process, but has been greatly accelerated by human activity. At present it is estimated that up to 100 species may become extinct every day. Most extinctions are caused by the destruction of habitat by humans. *See Biodiversity.*

Fish Stock - the number of fish of a particular species remaining in a particular ecosystem. Fishing is unsustainable if the rate of catching exceeds the ability of the stock to reproduce itself.

Fossil Fuels - carbon based compounds such as coal, oil and gas which were deposited or formed over millions of years and are now being exploited for use today. *See Greenhouse Effect, Global Warming, Climate Change and Greenhouse Gases.*

Genetic Engineering - the manipulation of genetic material (DNA) in a way that would not naturally occur. *See Biotechnology and Cloning.*

Global Warming - occurs when the atmosphere heats up as a consequence of the greenhouse effect. The impacts of global warming include climatic change and the rising of sea-levels as a result of the expansion of sea-water as it warms and the melting of land-based glaciers. *See Climate Change, Greenhouse Effect & Greenhouse Gases.*

Greenhouse Effect - the process whereby the earth's atmosphere is warmed as a consequence of an increase in the proportion of certain gases. The gases act like the glass in a greenhouse, allowing light energy from the sun to pass through to the surface of the earth. On striking the surface, some of the light energy is converted to heat (which is why you feel warm when you sit in the sun). This heat is absorbed by the greenhouse gases, so causing global warming. *See Climate Change, Greenhouse Gases & Global Warming.*

Greenhouse Gases - the main greenhouse gases are:
carbon dioxide - derived from the burning of fossil fuels;
methane - which is both naturally occurring and a consequence of certain animal husbandry practices;
CFCs - which are produced by human activity;
nitrous oxide - from the decomposition of nitrogenous organic matter.
See Climate Change, CFCs, Greenhouse Effect and Global Warming.

Hazardous Waste - material which poses a threat to life unless it is disposed of safely or treated successfully. There is particular concern over the disposal of chemical and nuclear waste material.

Herbicides- chemicals used to kill or minimise the growth of plant species. They are often applied to increase agricultural yields but their application, particularly if sustained over a long period or in high concentrations, can have a detrimental effect. *See Insecticides.*

Insecticides- chemicals used to kill insect species. The most well known is DDT. Many insecticides, like herbicides, may remain active for many years both in the soil and in the food chain. Their retention in the food chain means that they may have a detrimental impact on organisms for whom harm was not intended and in areas beyond where the insecticide was applied. Insecticides, as with herbicides, are used to gain benefits in agriculture and also to eradicate pests which may be a nuisance or harmful to human health. *See Herbicides.*

Nuclear Technology - the application of joining (fusion) or splitting (fission) of nuclear material to release energy in a controlled way, for example in a power station, or in an uncontrolled way, for example a nuclear bomb. Whilst every technology may have both benefits and risks attached, the impact of a nuclear accident may be particularly devastating because of the harmful and potentially long-term effects of radiation.

Organic Farming/Gardening - the process of farming or gardening without using man-made chemicals, which aims to maintain a healthy soil for future crops.

Ozone Layer - a naturally occurring layer around the upper atmosphere which acts to filter out harmful ultraviolet rays from the sun. During recent decades the ozone layer has been reduced, particularly above the poles, with the consequence that harmful rays have reached the earth. Ultra-violet rays are associated with the destruction of living cells which results in crop damage and, for humans, skin cancer and eye problems. The thinning of the ozone layer is mainly attributed to the release of chlorofluorocarbons (CFCs) from aerosols and refrigeration coolants. Fridges should therefore be disposed of through a Local Authority facility to ensure total destruction of the coolants rather than the release of CFCs. Whilst the Ozone Layer is vital as a filter at high altitude, from time to time, ozone builds up at a low level and can react with other atmospheric pollutants to produce smog, so reducing air-quality. *See CFCs.*

Pollution - occurs when substances are introduced into the environment that are either not naturally occurring or which are present in amounts exceeding natural levels. Pollution may be further categorised as atmospheric, water or land pollution.

Preservation - stabilising the state of a material or situation but not necessarily with respect to its original state. For example, fruit may be preserved as jam but the jam is rather different from the original fruit. Preservation is also a technique often applied to inanimate objects. For example, the National Trust preserves many of its buildings, but not necessarily as a living dynamic community. *See Conservation.*

Recycling - a process where things that people no longer have a use for can be re-used or turned into new products. For example the return of an empty milk bottle enables its re-use and taking waste glass to a bottle bank enables it to be turned into new glass products. Recycling can benefit the environment as it reduces the need for new raw materials, tends to use less energy than making things new, and reduces the need for land-fill sites and risk of pollution. *See Waste Minimisation and Pollution.*

Sustainable Development - the United Nations Commission on Environment and Development defined Sustainable Development as: *"Meeting the needs of the present without compromising the ability of future generations to meet their needs."* Sustainable Development should be distinguished from Sustainable Growth which is a term associated with Economics which has rather more to do with sustaining markets and consumerism than sustaining life!

Resources

Part 1: Useful contact addresses

House of Commons
London SW1A 0AA
0171 219 3000

Department of Environment
Transport and the Regions
Eland House, Bressenden Place
London SW1E 5DU
0171 890 3000

English Nature
Northminster House
Northminster Road
Peterborough
Cambridge PE1 1UA
01733 455000

The Environment Agency
Rio House
Waterside Drive
Almondsbury
Bristol BS12 4UD
01454 624400

Church and Conservation Project
Arthur Rank Centre
National Agricultural Centre
Stoneleigh Park
Warwickshire, CV8 2LZ
01203 696969
e-mail arthur.rank.centre@virgin.net

Friends of the Earth (England, Wales and Northern Ireland)
26-28 Underwood Street
London, N1 7JQ
0171 490 1555
e-mail info@foe.co.uk

Going for Green
Elizabeth House
The Pier
Wigan WN3 4EX
01942 612621
e-mail gfg@dircon.co.uk

Christian Ecology Link (CEL):
Information Officer
20 Carlton Road
Harrogate
North Yorkshire HG2 8DD
01423 871616

Membership Secretary
Christian Ecology Link
Freepost
204 Beulah Hill
London SE19 3BR
e-mail: info@christian-ecology.org.uk

Sacred Land Project
ICOREC
9a Didsbury Park
Manchester
M20 5LH

Friends of the Earth (Scotland)
Bonnington Mill
72 Newhaven Road
Edinburgh EH6 5QG

Note: **Going for Green** is an environmental awareness campaign which has entered into partnership with the Council of Churches for Britain and Ireland Environmental Issues Network to develop a Churches Environmental Project and an Eco-Church Award Scheme.

Part 2: Useful Material

Youth Resources

Causing a Stink The Eco Warriors Handbook, Caroline Clayton, Friends of the Earth £3.99
Rescue Mission Planet Earth A children's edition of Agenda 21, Kingfisher Books £6.99

Children's Resources *(commended by URC Children's Advocate Rosemary Johnston)*

Wonderful Earth, Nick Butterworth & Mick Inkpen, Hunt and Thorpe £9.99 (hardback)
Johnny Appleseed, Reeve Lindburgh, Little Brown publ. 1990
Anthology for the Earth, Judy Allen, Walker Books, 1997
paint a poem, Moira Andrew, Belair publ. 1996

Church Land and Property

Heating Your Church, William Bordass & Colin Bemrose, Church House Publishing £5.95
Heat and Light A practical guide to energy conservation in church buildings, Brian Marks, St Andrews Press £4.95
The Living Churchyard, Church and Conservation Project, Arthur Rank Centre (see above) £5

CEL Resources include:

Steps towards Sustainability pack of 18 leaflets on a range of practical topics, £4.
Car Free Days A Guide £2.50
Prayer Guide £6
How Green Is Your Church? 12 minutes video, £7.50
CEL annual membership costs £15 for which you will receive the journal Green Christians and the bulletin Caring for Creation.

Green Theology

The Earth Under Threat A Christian Perspective, Ghillean Prance, Wild Goose £6.99
God is Green, Ian Bradley, Darton, Longman & Todd, £6.95
The Environment & Christian Ethics, Michael Northcott, Cambridge University Press £15.95
Ecotheology A twice yearly journal of green theology, Sheffield Academic Press. £12

Environmental Issues

Three beautiful books of words with pictures of work by Pamela Pavitt: *Textures of Tomorrow (1997), Threads of Creation (1989), Leaves from the Tree of Peace (1986),* URC publ. £10 for three.
Textures of Tomorrow also in an educational pack, with posters, slides, etc. £13 inc p&p